CONTENTS

THE DAY BEFORE YOU

Words and Music by
MATTHEW WEST

Fsus2
C
you.
And I was read - y to set - tle for less
you.
But heav-en knows those years with - out you were
Am
Gsus2
than love and not much more. There was no such thing as a dream come true.
shap-ing my heart for the day that I found you, and if you're the rea - son for all I've been through,
Fsus2
Am
G5
3fr
Oh, but that was on the day be - fore you.
then I'm thank - ful for the day be - fore you.

Fsus2
C
Now you're here and
C/F
Am
G
ev - 'ry - thing's chang - ing. Sud - den - ly life means so
Fsus2
C
much. And I can't wait to
C/F
Am
G
wake up to - mor - row and find out this prom - ise is

F(add2)
D5
5fr
C/E
true. I will nev - er have to go back to
1
F(add2)
C
Csus
3fr
the day be - fore you.
C
Csus
3fr
2
F(add2)
G
the day be - fore
B♭sus2
3
you. And it was the last day that I ev - er lived a - lone,

F(add2)
and I'm nev - er go - ing back,
no, I'm nev - er go - ing back.
N.C.
D
Now you're here and
D/G
ev - 'ry - thing's chang - ing,
Bm
A
and sud - den - ly life means so
G(add2)
much.
D
And I can't wait to

G/B Bm A

wake up to - mor - row and find out this prom - ise is

G(add2) Em D/F♯

true. I will nev - er have to go back to,

G(add2) Em D/F♯

I will nev - er have to go back to

G(add2)

the day be - fore you,

D
Dsus
D
Dsus
the day be - fore you.
D/G
Gsus2
D/G
Gsus2
I'm nev - er go - ing back,
D
Dsus
D
Dsus
I'm nev - er go - ing back,
I'm nev - er go - ing back
D/G
Gsus2
Gsus2
to the day be - fore you.

DAY ONE

Words and Music by PETE KIPLEY
and MATTHEW WEST

Funky Rock groove

G5

I had a short-term mem-o-ry. Wish the on-ly thing my eyes could see was the fu-

Em7 Asus D5

-ture burn-ing bright right in front of me, but I can't stop look-ing back. Yeah, I wish

G5 D5 G5
3fr 5fr 3fr
I was a per - fect pic - ture of some - bod - y who's nev - er not good e - nough. Well, I try
Em7 Asus N.C.
to meas - ure up, but I mess it up, and I wish I was - n't like that. I
D G
wish I was - n't wish - ing an - y - more. Wish I could re - mem - ber that no - bod - y's keep - ing score. I'm tired
E5 N.C.
of throw - ing pen - nies in a well. I got - ta do some - thing; here goes noth - ing.

D
Gsus2
It's day one of the rest of my life.
It's day one of the
Em7
A7sus
D
best of my life.
I'm march - ing on to the beat of a
Gsus2
Em7
A7sus
To Coda
brand - new drum. Yeah, here I come.
The fu - ture has be - gun, day
D
D5
5fr
one.
Well, ev -

G5
3fr
- 'ry sin-gle day Your grace re-minds_ me that my best days are not be-hind_ me. Wher-
Em7
Asus
D5
5fr
ev-er my yes-ter-day may find_ me, well, I don't have to stay there,_ no.
G5
D5
G5
See, my ho-ur-glass is up-side down_ and my "some-day soon" is here_ and now._
Em7
Asus
D.S. al Coda
_ The clock is tick-ing and I'm so sick and tired of miss-ing out._ I

CODA
D
Bm
G
A7sus
D
one.
It's day _ one,
and here comes the _
Bm
G5
3fr
A5
5fr
D
G
D
_ sun.
Ev-'ry morn-ing,
ev-'ry morn-ing,
ev-'ry morn-ing mer-cy's _ new.
G
A
D
Ev-'ry morn-ing,
ev-'ry morn-ing,
I will fix my eyes on _ You.
G
A
D
Ev-'ry morn-ing,
ev-'ry morn-ing,
ev-'ry morn-ing mer-cy's _ new.

Bm
G
A7sus
D
Ev - 'ry morn - ing, ev - 'ry morn - ing, sun's com - ing up, the be - gin - ning has be - gun.
D
Yeah! It's day one of the rest of my life.
Gsus2
Em7
A7sus
D
It's day one of the best of my life. I'm march - ing
Gsus2
on to the beat of a brand - new drum. Yeah, here I come. The

1
2
Em7
A7sus
fu - ture has be - gun.
fu - ture has be - gun. (Start - ing
D
Gsus2
o - ver, I'm start - ing o - ver, start - ing o - ver, start - ing
Em7
A7sus
D
o - ver, start - ing now. I'm start - ing o - ver, I'm start - ing o - ver, start - ing
Gsus2
Em7
A7sus
D
o - ver, start - ing o - ver, start - ing now. I'm start - ing o - ver.)

FORGIVENESS

Words and Music by
MATTHEW WEST

C
op - po - site of how you feel when the pain they caused is just too real. Takes
F
ev - 'ry - thing you have to say the word. For - give - ness.
C
For - give - ness.
mf
F/C
It

C
flies in the face of all your pride, it moves a-way the mad in-side. It's
F/C
al-ways an-ger's own worst en-e-my.
C
E-ven when the ju-ry and the judge say you got a right to hold a grudge, it's the
F/C
whis-per in your ear say-ing, "Set it free." For-give-ness.

C
For - give - ness.
F
For - give - ness.
Am7
For - give - ness.
G
Show me how
cresc.

C
to love the un - lov - a - ble. Show me how
f
F
to reach the un - reach - a - ble. Help me now
Dm7
to do the im - pos - si - ble: for - give - ness.
C
For - give - ness.

F
Help me now
Dm7
F
to do the im - pos - si - ble: for - give - ness.
C5
3fr
It - 'll
dim.
mp
clear the bit - ter - ness a - way, it can e - ven set a pris - 'ner free. There

F
is no end to what its pow'r can do. So,
Am
let it go and be a - mazed by what you see through eyes of grace.
F
The pris - 'ner that it real - ly frees is you. For - give - ness.
C
For - give - ness.
building gradually

F
Oh, for - give -
Am
- ness.
For - give -
Gsus
3fr
- ness.
Show me how
C
to love the un - lov - a - ble.
Show me how
f

F
to reach the un - reach - a - ble.
Help me now
Dm7
to do the im - pos - si - ble:
F
for - give - ness.
C
I wan - na fi - nal - ly set it free,
so show me how
F
to see what Your mer - cy sees.
Help me now

Dm7
F
to give what You gave to me: for-give - ness.
C
Oh, for-give - ness.
F
For-give - ness.
C

F

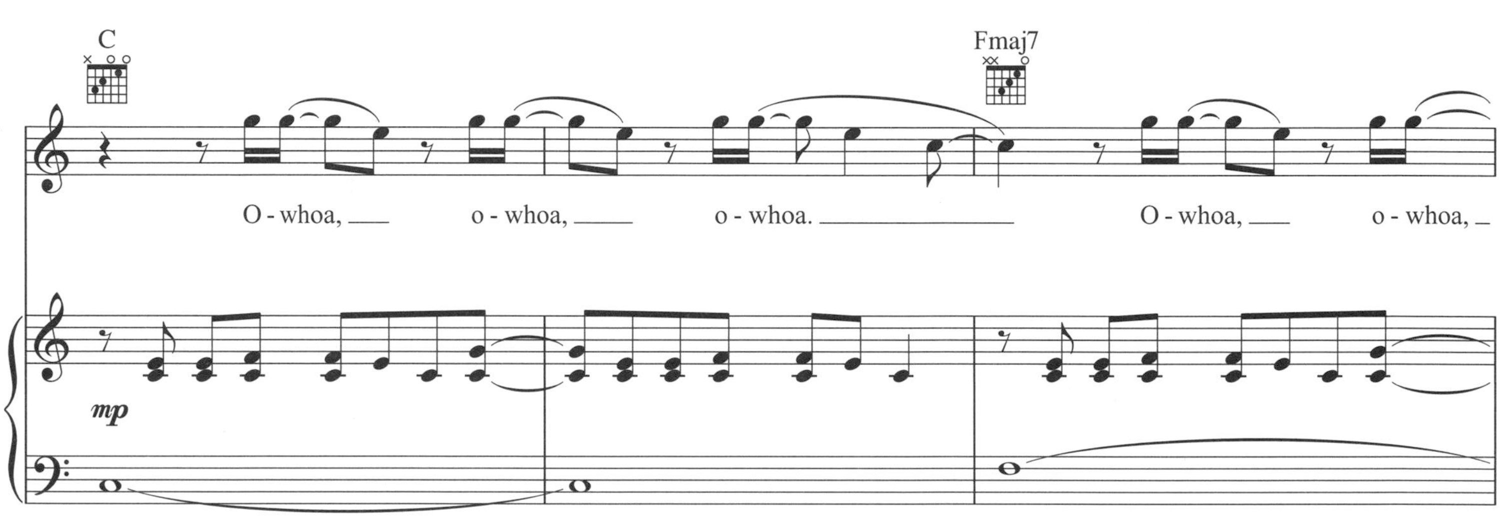
C
Fmaj7
O - whoa, o - whoa, o - whoa. O - whoa, o - whoa,
mp

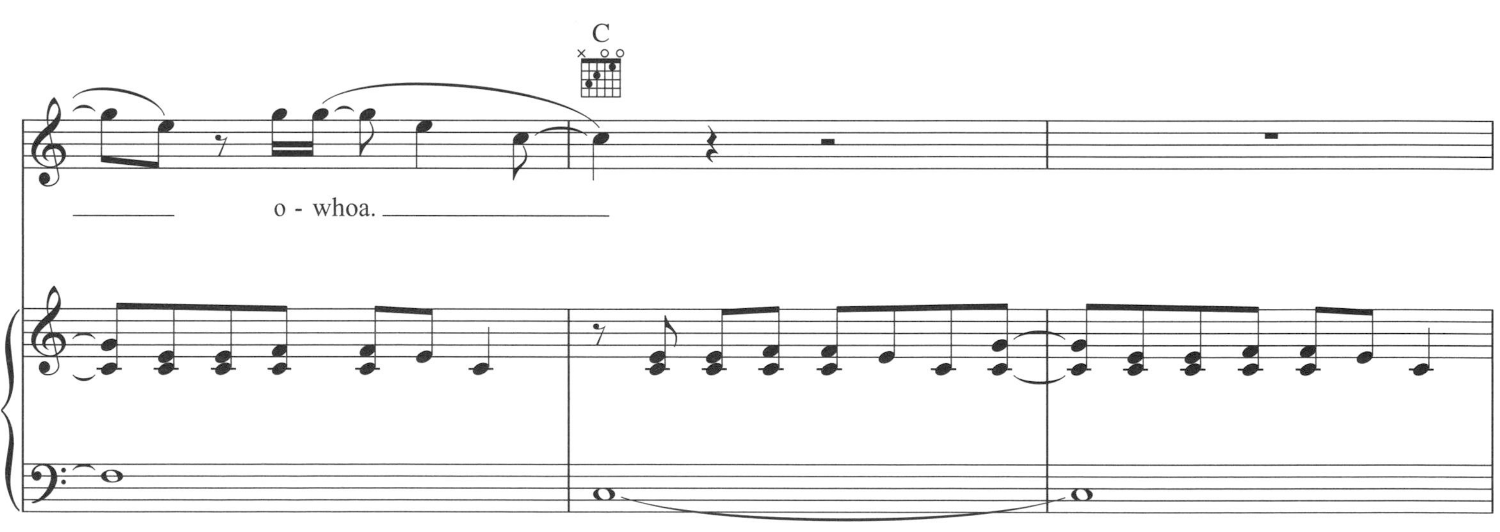
C
o - whoa.

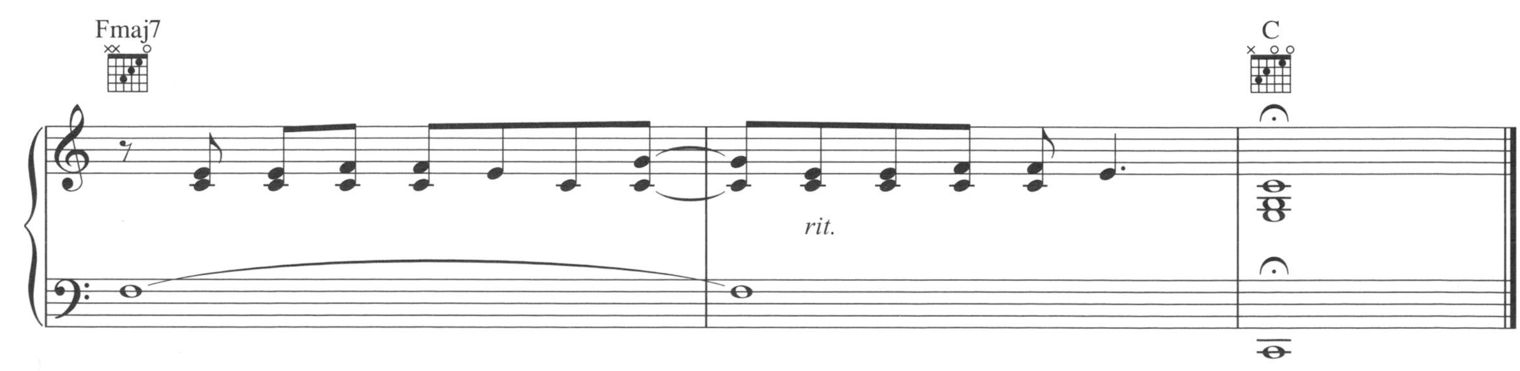
Fmaj7
C
rit.

DO SOMETHING

Words and Music by
MATTHEW WEST

Esus2
Asus2
how's it ev - er gon - na turn a - round?" _ So I turned my eyes to heav - en.
Esus2
I thought, "God, why don't You do ___ some - thing?"
E
Well, I just could - n't bear _ the thought _ of
Esus2
E
peo - ple liv - ing in pov - er - ty ___ and chil - dren sold in - to slav - er - y. ___

Esus2
Asus2
The thought dis - gust - ed me, so I shook my fist at heav - en.
Esus2
I said, "God, why don't You do some - thing?"
F♯m7
A6
He said, "I did." Yeah. "I cre - at - ed
E
you."

E
If not us, then who, if not me and
you right now?
A
Well, it's time for us to do
E
something, yeah.
If not now, then
when will we see an end to all this

A
C♯m
4fr
pain? Oh, it's not e - nough to do noth - ing.
To Coda
A
E
E7
It's time for us to do some-thing. (Na na na, na, na, na, na. na.
E
E7
Na, na, na, na, na, na, na, na.) I'm so tired of talk - ing a - bout
how we are God's hands and feet. But it's eas - i - er to say than to be,

Asus2
live like an - gels of ap - a - thy who tell our - selves,
E7
"It's all right. Some - bod - y else - 'll do some - thing."
Well, I don't know a - bout you,
but I'm sick and ti - red of life with no de - si - re. I

Asus2
don't want a flame; I want a fi - re.
I wan-na be the one who
E7
stands up and says, "I'm gon-na
do some - thing!"
D.S. al Coda
CODA
E
some - thing.
C♯m
4fr
We are the salt of the earth,
A
we are a cit - y on a hill.

E
(Shine, shine.
Shine, shine.)
C♯m
4fr
A
But we're nev - er gon - na change the world by stand - ing
B
still.
No, we won't stand still.
No, we won't stand still.
No, we won't stand

E
still, no.
If not us, then
who,
if not me and
you
right
A
now?
It's time for us to do
E
some - thing,

If not now, then when
will we see an end to all this
A
pain? Well, it's not e - nough to do
C♯m
nothing.
A
It's time for us to do

E
something. (Na, na, na, na.)
It's time for us to do
something. (Na, na, na, na.)
Ooh.
(Na, na, na, na.)
It's time for us to do
something. (Na, na, na, na.)

THE HEART OF CHRISTMAS

Words and Music by
MATTHEW WEST

A♭
4fr
E♭
3fr
The world's in a hur - ry thisDe - cem - ber,
D♭sus2
4fr
Fm7
the cit - y streets and shop - ping malls.
I wish we could slow down and re-
E♭
3fr
D♭sus2
4fr
mem - ber the mean - ing of it all.
Wher -
A♭
4fr
E♭
3fr
B♭m7
ev - er you are, no mat - ter how far, come back to the heart, the
mf

D♭sus2
A♭
E♭
heart of Christ - mas. Live while you can, cher - ish the mo - ment; and the
B♭m7
D♭
Fm7
To Coda
ones that you love, make sure they know it. And don't
E♭
B♭m7
A♭/D♭
miss it: the heart of Christ - mas.
A♭
E♭
B♭m7

Ab/Db
Ab
Eb/G
Let's make it feel the way it used to,
Dbsus2
Ab
let's find the won - der of a child.
You could see the mag - ic all a - round
Eb/G
Dbsus2
you; come on and o - pen up your eyes.
Ab
Eb/G
You can find it in the warm em - brace of your fam - i - ly

D♭sus2
4fr
Fm7
or call - ing up a long - lost friend.
You can e - ven find it in the
E♭
3fr
D♭sus2
4fr
D.S. al Coda
eyes of a stran - ger
when you reach out a help - ing hand.
Wher-
CODA
E♭/G
3fr
B♭m7
D♭sus2
4fr
miss it: the heart of Christ - mas.
Fm7
A♭
4fr
In the shad - ow of a stee - ple, in a star
f

D♭
A♭
4fr
that lights the way. You will find Him in a man-
E♭
3fr
- ger; the heart of Christ - mas has a name.
A♭
4fr
E♭
3fr
D♭sus2
4fr
I'm gon-na make a wish this Christ - mas,
I'm gon-na say a lit-tle prayer.
mp
A♭
4fr
E♭
3fr
Wher - ev - er you are, no mat - ter how far, come

D♭
E♭sus
6fr
A♭
4fr
back to the heart, the heart of Christ - mas. Live while you can and
gradual cresc.
E♭
3fr
B♭m7
D♭
cher-ish the mo - ment; and the ones that you love, make sure they know it. Wher -
A♭
4fr
E♭
3fr
B♭m7
ev - er you are, no mat - ter how far, come back to the heart, the
f
D♭
A♭
4fr
E♭
3fr
heart of Christ - mas. Live while you can, cher - ish the mo - ment; and the

B♭m7
D♭
ones that you love, make sure they know it. And
Fm7
E♭/G
B♭m7
3fr
don't miss it: the heart of
D♭sus2
4fr
A♭
4fr
Christ - mas.
mp
E♭/G
3fr
D♭/F
D♭sus2
4fr
rit.

HELLO, MY NAME IS

Words and Music by
MATTHEW WEST

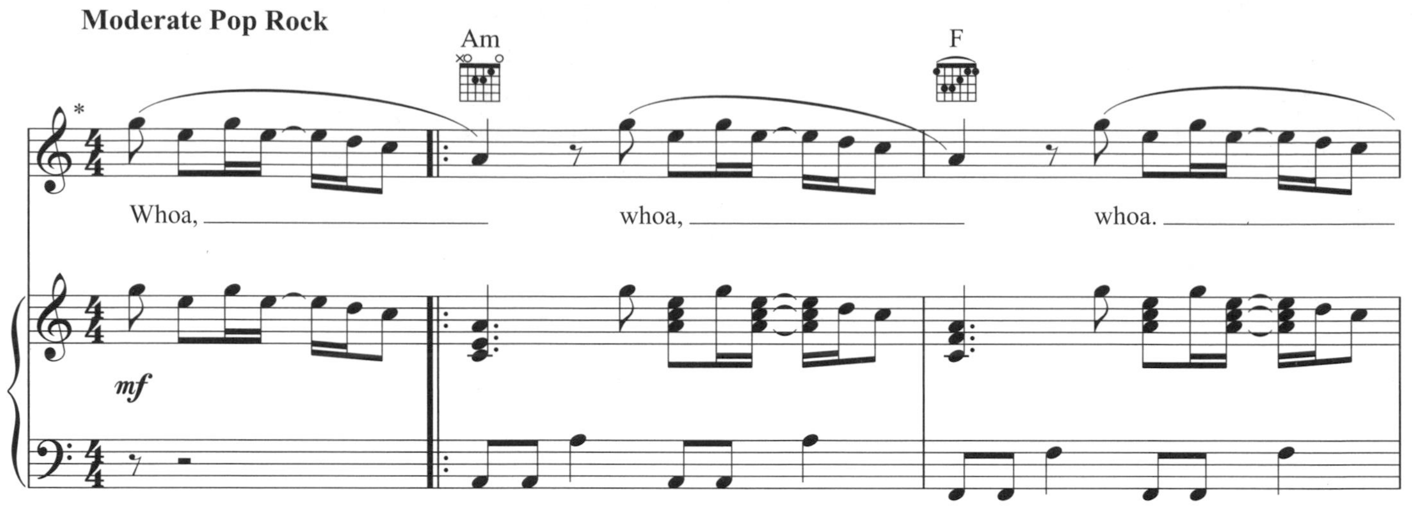

* Recorded a half step lower.

F
Ev - 'ry sin - gle day of your life,
I'm the whis - per in - side
Dm
that won't let you for - get.
C
N.C.
Hel - lo, my name is De - feat.
C
I know you rec - og - nize me.
Am

F
Just when you think you can win, I'll drag you right back down a - gain
Dm
C
till you've lost all be - lief.
Am
Am9
5fr
Oh, these are the voic - es,
Am7
F
Cmaj7/F
oh, these are the lies.

F
Dm7
And I have be - lieved them
G
for the ver - y last time.
C
Hel - lo, my name is Child of the One True King.
F
I've been saved, I've been changed, I have been set free.

Dm
F
"A - maz - ing Grace" is the song I sing. Hel - lo, my name is
C
Am
To Coda
Child of the One True King. Whoa, whoa,
F
C
N.C.
whoa. I am no long - er de -
C
Am
- fined by all the wreck - age be - hind.

F
Dm
The One who makes all things new has prov- en it's true; just take a look at my life.
C
G
D.S. al Coda
Hel- lo, my name is
CODA
F
whoa.
C
What love the
Am
Fa- ther has lav - ished up - on us, that we should be called His chil-

F
C
-dren. I am a child of the one true_ King. What love the
Am
Fa-ther has lav-ished up-on us, that we should be called_ His chil-
F
C
-dren. Hel-lo, my name_ is Child of the One True_ King.
F
I've been saved, I've been changed, I have been set_ free. "A-maz-ing_ Grace"_

Dm
F
C
is the song I sing. Hel - lo, my name is Child of the One True King.
Am
F
Whoa, whoa, whoa.
C
I am a child of the one true King.
Whoa,
Am
F
C
whoa, whoa.

MENDED

Words and Music by
MATTHEW WEST

Gm
Eb
Bb
Gm
Oh, but I can still rec - cog-nize the one I love in your
Eb
Bb/D
Gm
Eb
Bb
tear - stained eyes. I know you might not see it now, so
F
Ebsus2
lift your eyes to Me. When you see bro -
Bb
Ebsus2
- ken be - yond re - pair, I see heal - ing be - yond be - lief.

Gm7
When you see too far gone,
I see one
E♭sus2
6fr
step a - way from home.
B♭
You see noth - ing but dam - aged goods,
Dm
I see some - thing good in the mak - ing.
I'm not
Gm7
fin - ished yet.
E♭sus2
6fr
When you see wound - ed,
To Coda

Gm
E♭sus2
Fsus
I see mend - ed.
mf
Gm
E♭sus2
B♭
Gm
You see your
E♭
B♭
Gm
E♭
B♭
worst mis-take, but I see the price I paid.
Gm
E♭
B♭
And there's noth - ing you could ev - er do to

F
Eb
3fr
Gm
3fr
lose what grace has won.
So hold on, it's
Eb
3fr
Bb
Gm
3fr
Eb
3fr
Bb
not the end.
No, this is where love's work be - gins.
Gm
3fr
Eb
3fr
Bb
F
I'm mak - ing all things new, and I will make a
Ebsus2
6fr
D.S. al Coda
mir - a - cle of you.
When you see bro -

CODA
B♭
I see mend - ed.
I see My child,
mf
Gm
3fr
My be - lov - ed, the new cre - a - tion you're be - com -
E♭sus2
6fr
- ing. You see the scars from when you fell,
but I see the sto -
Dm
- ries they will tell.
You see worth - less, but I see price -

E♭sus2
6fr
- less. You see pain, but I see a pur - pose. You see un -
B♭
F
worth - y, un - de - serv - ing, but I see you through eyes
of mer - cy. When you see bro -
B♭
E♭sus2
6fr
- ken be - yond re - pair, I see heal - ing be - yond be - lief.
mp

Gm7
You're not too far gone, you're one
cresc.
E♭sus2
6fr
B♭
step a - way from home. When you see noth - ing but dam - aged goods,
f
Dm
I see some - thing good in the mak - ing. I'm not
Gm7
F
E♭sus2
6fr
fin - ished yet, no. When you see wound - ed,

B♭
I see mend - ed.
Oh,
Dm7
Gm7
I see mend - ed.
E♭
3fr
Whoa, oh, I see mend - ed.
B♭
Dm

Gm7
F
I'm not fin - ished yet.
When
E♭sus2
6fr
B♭
you see wound - ed, I see mend - ed.
Gm
3fr
E♭
3fr
B♭
Gm
3fr
E♭
3fr
B♭
mp
Gm
3fr
E♭
3fr
B♭
Gm
3fr
mp sub.

MORE

Words and Music by KENNY GREENBERG,
JASON HOUSER and MATTHEW WEST

F/A
F
A5
5fr
think of Me.
Take a look at the de - sert;
Just a face in the cit - y,
C
F
A5
5fr
do you feel like a grain of sand?
I am with you wher - ev - er;
just a tear on a crowd - ed street,
but you are one in a mil - lion
C
B♭
where you go is where I am,
and I'm al - ways
and you be - long to Me.
And I
A♭
4fr
B♭
A♭
4fr
B♭
think - ing of you.
Take a look a - round you;
I'm
want you to know
that I'm not let - ting go,

A♭
4fr
B♭
F
spell - ing it out one by one.
e - ven when you come un - done.
C5
3fr
Fsus2
I love you more than the sun and the stars that I taught how to shine.
Am
F5
C5
3fr
You are Mine and you shine for Me, too. I love you yes - ter - day and to - day
Fsus2
Am
Gsus
3fr
G
and to - mor - row. I'll say it a - gain and a - gain. I love you

F5
Am
C5
3fr
more.
1
I love you more,
yeah.
2
Dm
C/E
Shine for Me.
Fsus2
You shine for Me.
You shine on,

C/E
A♭5
4fr
B♭sus2
you shine on, you shine for Me.
D5
5fr
Gsus2
I love you more than the sun and the stars that I taught how to shine.
Bm
G5
3fr
D5
5fr
You are Mine and you shine for Me, too.
I love you yes-ter-day and to-day
I love you yes-ter-day and to-day,
Gsus2
1
Bm
Asus
A
and to-mor-row. I'll say it a-gain and a-gain. I love you
through the joy and the pain.

2
Bm
Asus
A
I'll say it a - gain and a - gain.
I love you
G5
3fr
Bm
D5
5fr
more.
I love you more.
And I see you, and I made you,
and I love you more than you can i - mag -

G
B5
D
-ine, more than you can fath-om. I love
you more than the sun, and you shine for
Me.
Repeat and Fade
Optional Ending
D5
5fr

GRACE WINS

Words and Music by
MATTHEW WEST

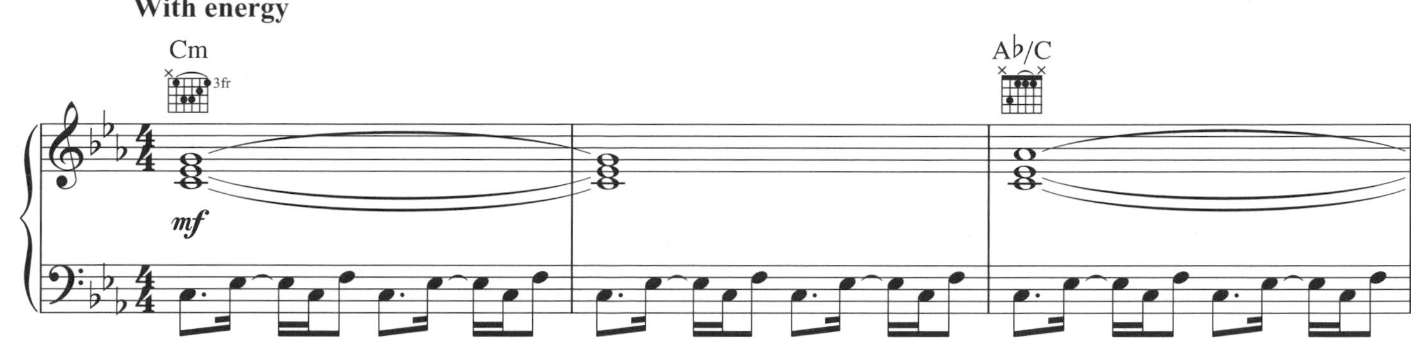

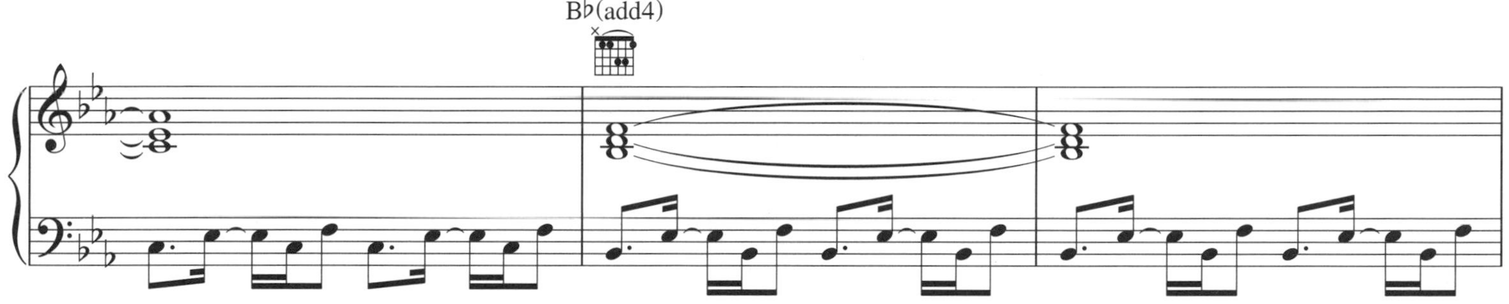

A♭(add2)
4fr
B♭
grace.
I can read the dis - ap-point - ment
Fm
writ-ten all o - ver Your face.
N.C.
Cm7
3fr
Here come those whis - pers in my ear,
A♭
4fr
say - ing, "Who do you think you are?
Looks like you're on your own from

B♭
Fm
here, 'cause grace could nev-er reach that far.
N.C.
A♭
E♭
But in the shad-ow of that shame, beat down by all the
Cm
B♭
blame, I hear You call my name, say-ing, "It's not o-ver." And
A♭
E♭
Cm
my heart starts to beat so loud now, drown-ing out the doubt. I'm down, but I'm not

B♭
E♭
3fr
out. There's a war be - tween guilt and grace, and they're
A♭
4fr
B♭
fight - ing for a sa - cred space. But I'm liv - ing proof:
A♭
4fr
E♭
3fr
A♭sus2
3fr
E♭
3fr
A♭sus2
3fr
grace wins ev - 'ry time. No more
E♭
3fr
A♭
4fr
ly - ing down in death's de - feat. Now I'm ris - ing up in

B♭
A♭
4fr
vic - to - ry, sing - ing: Hal - le - lu - jah! Grace wins ev - 'ry time.
To Coda
E♭
3fr
A♭sus2
3fr
E♭
3fr
Cm
3fr
Words can't de - scribe the way it feels
A♭maj7
when mer - cy floods a thirst - y soul,
the broke in - side be - gins to
B♭
Fm7
heal
and grace re - turns what guilt - y stole.

A♭
E♭
And in the shad-ow of my shame, beat down by all the
Cm
B♭
blame, I hear You call my name, say-ing, "It's not o-ver." And
A♭
E♭
Cm
my heart starts to beat so loud now, drown-ing out the doubt. I'm down, but I'm not
B♭
D.S. al Coda
out. There's a
CODA
E♭
A♭sus2
3fr
E♭
For the prod-i-gal son,

A♭sus2
3fr
grace wins. For the wom-an at the well, grace wins. For the
Cm7
3fr
blind man and the beg-gar, grace wins.
A♭sus2
3fr
For al-ways and for-ev - er,
grace wins. For the
E♭
lost out on the street, grace wins. For the
A♭sus2
3fr
worst part of you and me, grace wins. For the
Cm7
3fr
thief on the cross,

A♭sus2
3fr
grace wins. For a world that is lost. There's a
E♭
3fr
A♭
4fr
war be-tween guilt and grace, and they're fight - ing for a
B♭
A♭
4fr
sa - cred space. But I'm liv - ing proof: grace wins ev - 'ry time.
E♭
3fr
A♭sus2
3fr
E♭
3fr
A♭sus2
3fr
E♭
3fr
No more ly - ing down in

A♭
4fr
death's de - feat. Now I'm ris - ing up in vic - to - ry, sing - ing:
B♭
A♭
4fr
E♭
3fr
A♭sus2
3fr
Hal - le - lu - jah! Grace wins ev - 'ry time,
E♭
3fr
A♭sus2
3fr
ev - 'ry time.
Yeah, I'm
B♭
A♭sus2
3fr
E♭
3fr
liv - ing proof: grace wins ev - 'ry time.
rit.

THE MOTIONS

Words and Music by SAM MIZELL,
MATTHEW WEST and JASON HOUSER

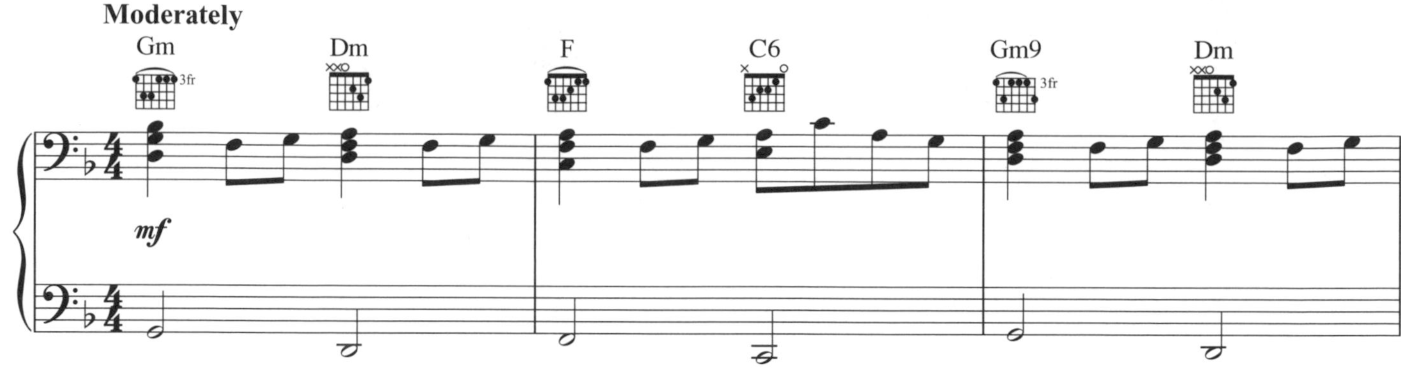

F
C
Gm
3fr
Dm
at least I'll be feel - ing some - thing. 'Cause "just o - kay" is not e - nough.
I think I'm fi - n'lly feel - ing some - thing. 'Cause "just o - kay" is not e - nough.
F
C
B♭
Help me fight through the noth - ing - ness of life.
Help me fight through the noth - ing - ness of this life.
Dm
F
C
Gm
3fr
I don't wan - na go through the mo - tions. I don't wan - na go one more day
Dm
F
C
with - out Your all - con - sum - ing pas - sion in - side of me.

Gm
3fr
Dm
F
C
I don't wan - na spend my whole life ask - ing, "What if I had giv - en ev - 'ry -
B♭
1
Gm9
3fr
Dm
- thing in - stead of go - ing through the mo - tions?" _
F
C6
Gm9
3fr
Dm
F
C6
2
Gm
3fr
B♭
F
C
go - ing through the mo - tions?" ___ (Take me all the way.) ___ Take me all the way. ____

Gm
B♭
F
C
3fr
(Take me all the way.) 'Cause I don't wan - na go through the mo - tions.
Gm
B♭
F
C
3fr
(Take me all the way.) Now I'm fi - nal - ly feel - ing some - thing
Gm
B♭
F
Csus
3fr
real. (Take me all the way.)
Dm
F
C
Gm
3fr
I don't wan - na go through the mo - tions. I don't wan - na go one more day

Dm
F
C
with - out Your all - con - sum - ing pas - sion in - side of me.
Gm
3fr
Dm
F
C
I don't wan - na spend my whole life ask - ing, "What if I had giv - en ev - 'ry -
B♭
- thing in - stead of go - ing through the mo - tions?"
Dm
F
C
Gm
3fr
I don't wan - na go through the mo - tions. I don't wan - na go one more day

Dm
F
C
with - out Your all - con - sum - ing pas - sion in - side of me.
Gm
3fr
Dm
F
C
I don't wan - na spend my whole life ask - ing, "What if I had giv - en ev - 'ry - thing
B♭
Gm
3fr
B♭
in - stead of go - ing through the mo - tions?" (Take me all the way.)
F
C
Gm
3fr
B♭
Take me all the way. (Take me all the way.)

F
Gm
3fr
B♭
I don't wan - na go, I don't wan - na go through the mo -

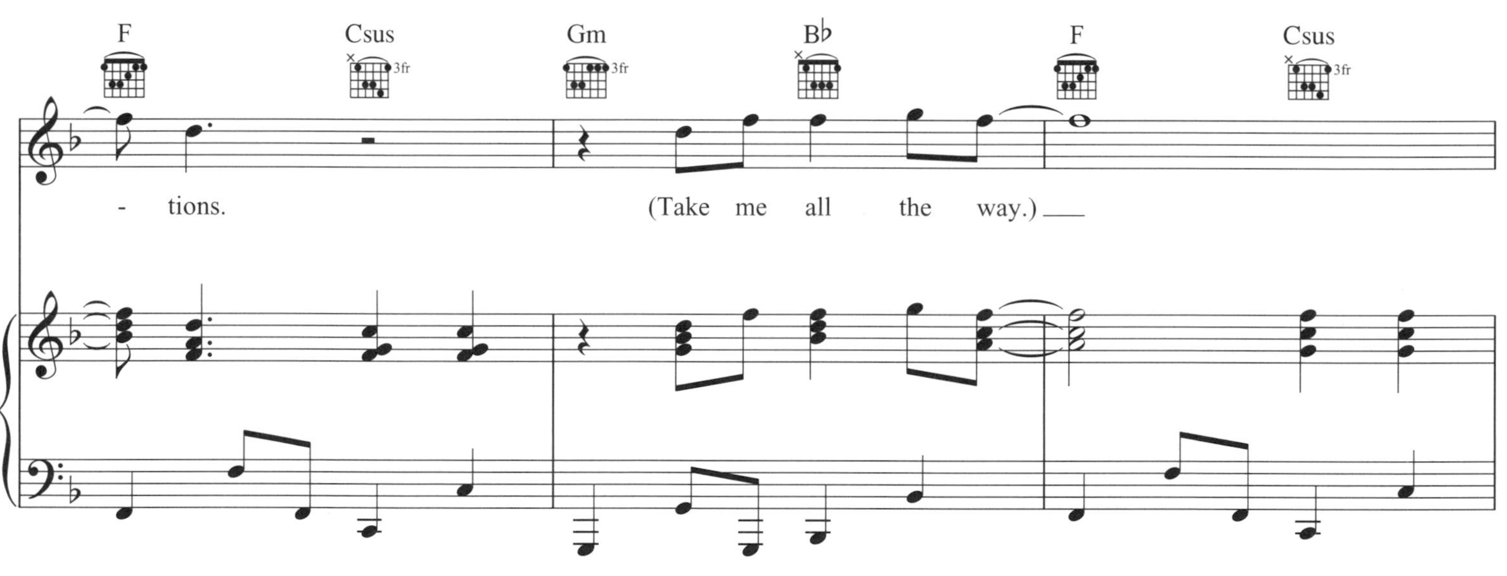
F
Csus
3fr
Gm
3fr
B♭
F
Csus
3fr
- tions. (Take me all the way.)

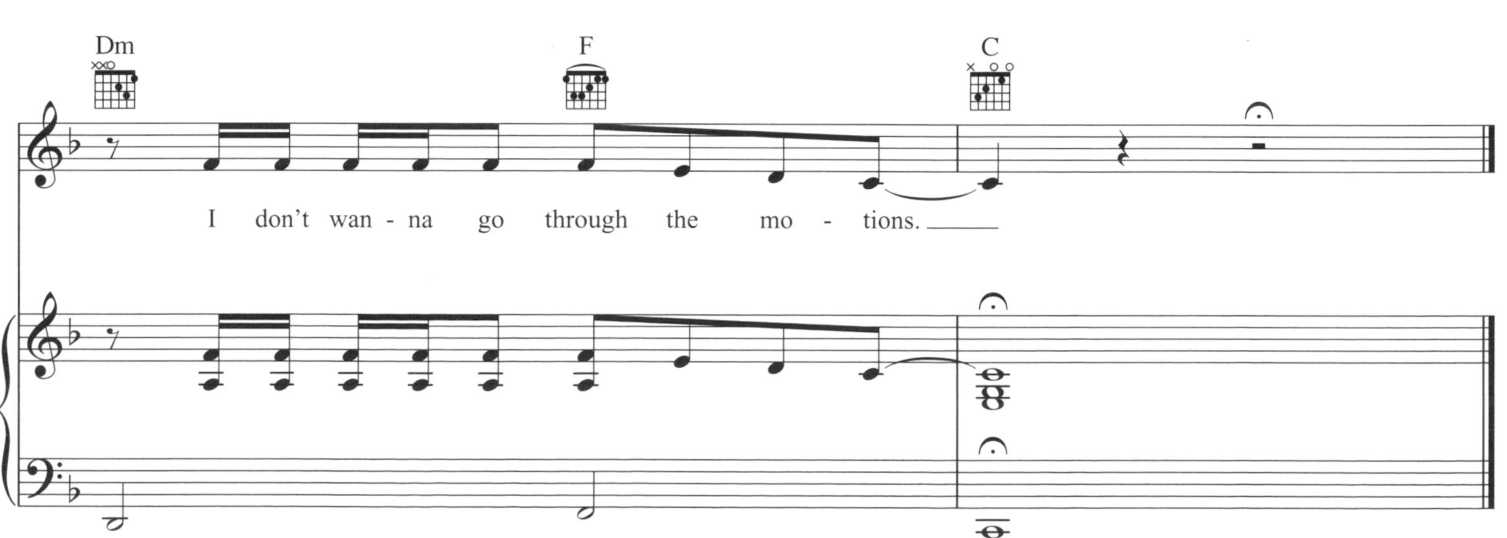
Dm
F
C
I don't wan - na go through the mo - tions.

MY OWN LITTLE WORLD

Words and Music by
MATTHEW WEST

* Recorded a half step lower.

Bm
D
Gsus2
own lit - tle world, pop - u - la - tion: me. I
Bm
Gsus2
D
try to stay a - wake dur - ing Sun - day morn - ing church. I throw a
Bm
Gsus2
D
twen - ty in the plate, but I nev - er give till it hurts. And I turn
Bm
G
D
off the news when I don't like what I see. It's eas -

Bm
D
Gsus2
A
Bm7
-y to do when it's pop-u-la - tion: me.
What if there's a big-ger pic-ture?
G
D
A
Bm7
What if I'm miss - ing out?
What if there's a great - er pur - pose
G
D
Gsus2
D
A
I could be liv-ing right now,
out-side my own lit-tle world?
Gsus2
D
A
N.C.
Ooh.
Stopped at a red light, looked out my win -

D
Bm
G
dow. I saw a card-board sign, said, "Help this home - less wid - ow."
D
Bm
G
And just a - bove that sign was the face of a hu -
D
Bm
D
man. I thought to my - self, "God, what have I been do - ing?"
Gsus2
Bm
G
So I rolled down the win - dow and I looked her in the eye.

D
Bm
G
D
Oh, how many-y times have I just passed her by?
I gave
Bm
G
D
her some mon-ey, then I drove on through,
and my
Bm
D
Gmaj7
own lit-tle world reached pop-u-la-tion: two.
Oh,
A
Bm7
G
D
what if there's a big-ger pic-ture?
What if I'm miss-ing out?

A
Bm7
G
D
What if there's a great - er pur - pose that I could be liv - ing right now,
Gsus2
D
A
G
D
out - side my own lit - tle world? Ooh.
A
G
D
A
Asus
My own lit - tle world, ooh.
Dsus
D
G
Dsus
D
Whoa, whoa,

A
Dsus
D
G
whoa.
Bm
Gsus2
D
Fa - ther, break my heart for what breaks Yours.
Give me
Bm
Gsus2
D
Bm
Gsus2
o - pen hands and o - pen doors.
Put Your light in my eyes and let me see
D
Bm
D
Gsus2
that my own lit - tle world is not a - bout me.

A
Bm7
G
D
What if there's a big - ger pic - ture?
What if I'm miss - ing out?
A
Bm7
G
D
What if there's a great - er pur - pose
that I could be liv - ing right now?
A
Bm7
Gsus2
D
I don't wan - na miss what mat - ters,
I wan - na be reach - ing out.
A
Bm7
Gsus2
D
Show me the great - er pur - pose
so I can start liv - ing right now

Gsus2
D
A
Gsus2
D
out - side my own lit - tle world,
ooh.
A
Gsus2
D
A
My own lit - tle world,
yeah,
yeah.
My own lit - tle world,
G
D
A
Dsus
D
G
ooh.
Whoa,
Dsus
D
A
Dsus
D
G
whoa,
whoa.

ONLY GRACE

Words and Music by KENNETH GREENBERG
and MATTHEW WEST

F
Cm7
3fr
The dirt has washed a - way, and now it's clear.
E♭sus2
6fr
B♭
There's on - ly grace, there's on - ly
Fsus
E♭
3fr
love, there's on - ly mer - cy, and be - lieve me, it's e - nough.
Gm7
Your sins are gone with - out a trace,

F
Cm7
3fr
and there's noth - ing left now, there's on - ly
Ebmaj7
3fr
To Coda
grace.
Gm7
Ebsus2
6fr
mf
F
Bb
You're start - ing o - ver now, un - der the
Gm7
F
sun. You're step - ping for - ward now; a new life has be - gun.

E♭
D.S. al Coda
Your new life has be - gun.
And there's on - ly
cresc.
CODA
E♭
Gm
E♭
And if you should fall a - gain, well, get back up,
F
E♭
Gm
E♭
get back up. Reach out and take my hand and get back up,
F
E♭
and get back up, and get back up a - gain. Oh,

B♭
get back up a - gain. There's on - ly grace, there's on - ly love,
mf
Fsus
E♭
3fr
there's on - ly mer - cy, and be - lieve me, it's e -
3
nough, it's e - nough. Your sins are gone with - out a trace,
Gm7
F
Cm7
and there's noth - ing left now, there's on - ly,

E♭
B♭
there's on - ly
grace.
Fsus
E♭
There's on - ly mer - cy, and be - lieve me, it's e - nough,
Gm7
it's e - nough. Your sins are gone with - out a trace,
F
Cm7
and there's noth - ing left now, there's on - ly

E♭
3fr
grace.
Gm7
E♭sus2
6fr
F
So get back up, and get back up
Gm7
E♭sus2
6fr
F
a - gain.
Get back up
E♭
3fr
Gm7
F
E♭sus2
6fr
Gm7
F
a - gain.
mf

SAVE A PLACE FOR ME

Words and Music by SAM MIZELL
and MATTHEW WEST

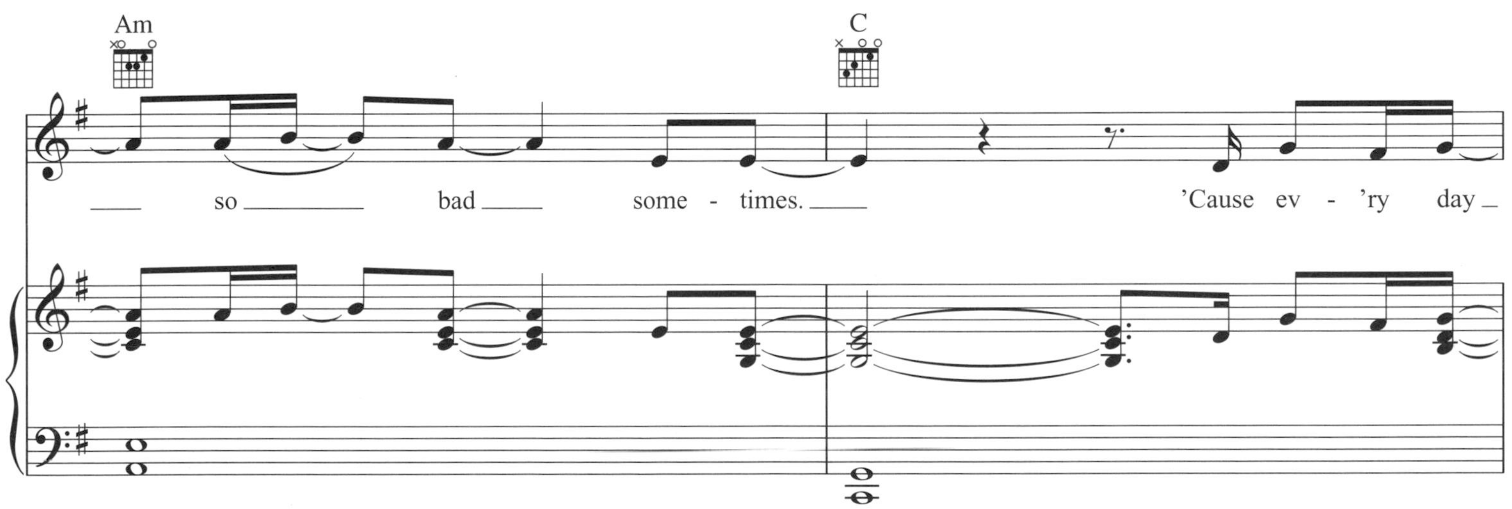

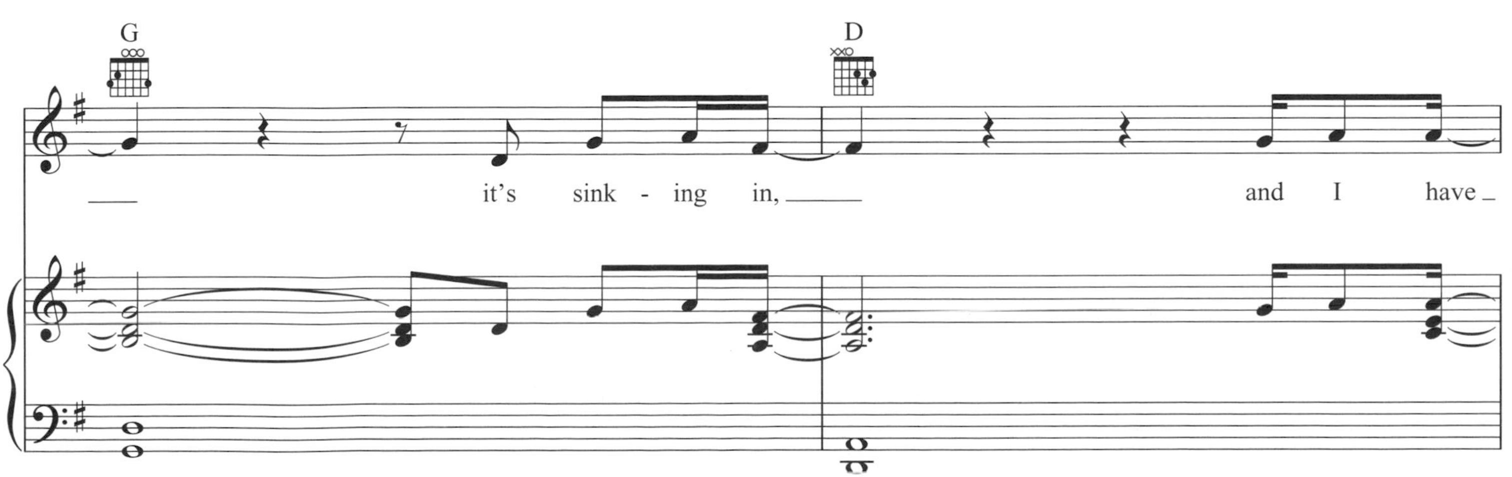

Am
C
to say good-bye all o - ver a - gain.
You know, I
D
Em
C
bet it feels good to have the weight of this world off your shoul - ders now.
I'm
D
Em
Csus2
3fr
dream-ing of the day when I'm fi - nal - ly there with you.
G
D
Save a place for me,
save a place for me,
save a place for me.

Am
C
I'll be there soon, I'll be there soon.
G
D
Save a place for me, save some grace for me.
To Coda
Am
C
Fsus2
I'll be there soon, I'll be there soon.
G
D
La da da, la da da. La da da da da da da.

Am
C
G
I have asked the questions
D
Am
why, but I guess the an - swer's for an - oth - er time.
C
G
So in - stead, I'll pray with ev - 'ry
D
Am
tear, and be thank - ful for the time I had you

C
D.S. al Coda
CODA
C
here. So you just
I'll be there.
D
Em
Csus2
3fr
I wan-na live my life just like you did,
D
Em
Csus2
Csus2(♯4)
Csus2
and make the most of my time just like you did. And I wan-na make
D
Em
Csus2
my home up in the sky, just like you did. Oh,

but un - til I get there,
un - til I get there, just
G
D
save a place for me,
save a place for me,
Am9
5fr
C
N.C.
G
'cause I will be there soon.
D
Am7
G/B
Csus2
3fr

G
D
Save a place for me,
save a place for me.
Am
C
Fsus2
I'll be there soon,
I'll be there soon.
G
D
La da da,
la da da.
La da da
da
da
da
da.
Am
C
Fsus2
G
La da da,
la da da.
La da da
da
da
da
da.

STRONG ENOUGH

Words and Music by
MATTHEW WEST

A
D
Well, for - give me, for - give me if I'm wrong,
F♯m7
E
but this looks like more than I can do on
Bm
N.C.
A
my own.
I know I'm not strong e - nough to be
D
F♯m7
ev - 'ry - thing that I'm sup - posed to be. I give up; I'm not

D
A
strong e - nough.
Hands of mer - cy, won't you cov - er me?
D
F♯m7
To Coda
Lord, I'm ask - ing now for You to be strong e - nough,
E
A
strong e - nough for the both of us.
Yeah.
D
F♯m7

D
A
Well, may - be, may -
D
F♯m7
- be that's the point:
to reach the point of giv -
D
A
ing up.
'Cause when I'm fi - n'lly,
D
F♯m7
fi - n'lly at rock bot - tom,
well, that's when I start look -

E
Bm
D.S. al Coda
- ing up and reach - ing out.
CODA
E
G
strong e - nough. 'Cause I'm bro - ken down to noth - ing. But I'm still
F♯m7
hold-ing on to the one thing: You are God and You are strong when
D
A
I am weak. I can do all

E
A
D
things through Christ who gives me strength.
F#m7
E
A/C#
I don't have to be strong e - nough, strong e - nough.
Dsus2
A
Esus
I can do all things through
A/C#
D
Christ who gives me strength, and I don't have to be

Dsus2
strong e - nough, _
A/C♯
D
_ strong e - nough. _
A
Dsus2
F♯m
Oh, _
yeah. _
Dsus2
A
_
I know I'm not strong e - nough _ to be

D
F♯m7
ev - 'ry - thing that I'm sup - posed_ to be. I give up; I'm not
D
A
strong e - nough.
Hands of mer - cy, won't you cov - er me?
D
F♯m7
Lord, right now I'm ask - ing You_ to be strong e - nough,
E/G♯
Bm7
Dsus2
strong e - nough, strong e - nough.

YOU ARE EVERYTHING

Words and Music by MATTHEW WEST
and SAM MIZELL

Gm7
E♭sus2
6fr
B♭
F
ev - 'ry time You look at me, I'm spin - ning like an au - tumn leaf,
Gm
3fr
E♭
3fr
B♭
F
E♭sus2
6fr
bound to hit bot - tom some - time. Where would I be with-out
Fsus
F
some - one to save me, some - one who won't let me fall?
B♭
Gm7
You are ev - 'ry - thing that I live for,

F
— ev - 'ry - thing that I can't be - lieve is hap - pen - ing. You're
E♭
3fr
stand - ing right in front of me with arms wide o - pen. All I know is,
B♭
ev - 'ry day is filled with hope 'cause You are — ev - 'ry - thing that I
Gm7
Fsus
breathe for, — and I can't help but breathe You in and breathe a - gain,

To Coda
F
E♭
3fr
feel - ing all this life with - in,
ev - 'ry sin - gle beat of my
heart.
Gm7
E♭sus2
6fr
B♭
F7
Gm7
E♭sus2
6fr
B♭
F7
Gm7
E♭sus2
6fr
B♭
F/A
I'm the one with big mis - takes,
big re - grets and big - ger breaks than

Gm
3fr
E♭
3fr
B♭
F/A
I'd ev - er care to con - fess.
Oh, but
Gm7
E♭sus2
6fr
B♭
F
You're the One who looks at me and sees what I was meant to be,
Gm
3fr
E♭
3fr
B♭
F
D.S. al Coda
more than just a beau - ti - ful mess.
CODA
A♭
4fr
ev - 'ry sin - gle beat of my heart.
You're

E♭
B♭/D
Cm7
E♭
B♭/D
ev - 'ry-thing good in my life, ev - 'ry - thing hon-est and
Cm
E♭
B♭/D
Cm
B♭
true, and all of those stars hang - ing up in the sky could
A♭
Fsus
B♭
nev - er shine bright - er than You... are
Gm7
ev - 'ry - thing that I live for, ev - 'ry - thing that I

F
can't be - lieve is hap - pen - ing. You're stand - ing right in front of me with
E♭
3fr
arms wide o - pen. All I know is, ev - 'ry day is filled with hope 'cause
B♭
You are ev - 'ry - thing that I
Gm7
breathe for,
and I can't help but
Fsus
breathe You in and breathe a - gain,

F
Eb
3fr
feel - ing all this life with - in, ev - 'ry sin - gle beat of my heart.
Gm7
Ebsus2
6fr
Bb
F7
You are, oh, You are,
Je - sus, You are,
Eb(add2)
You are ev - 'ry - thing.

WHEN I SAY I DO

Words and Music by
MATTHEW WEST

* Recorded a half step lower.

C
G
F
Am
plan for this cra - zy life, be-cause He brought you
C
Fsus2
G
here and placed you by my side. And I have
F
C
Am
G
nev-er been so sure of an - y-thing be-fore like I am
F
C
G
in this mo - ment here with you. And now "for

F
C
Am
G
bet - ter or for worse" are so much more than on - ly words, and I pray
Dm
Am
ev - 'ry day will be the proof that I mean
F
C
G
Am
what I say when I say, "I do." Yeah, I mean
F
C
To Coda
G
Am
C
G
what I say when I say "I do." Oh.

F
Am
C
F
G
Am
You see, these hands you
C
G
F
Am
hold will al - ways hold you up when the strength you
C
Fsus2
G
Am
have just ain't strong e - nough. And what to - mor - row
C
G
F
Am
brings, on - ly time will tell, but I will stand by

D.S. al Coda
C
Fsus2
G
C/E
you in sick-ness and in health. 'Cause I have
CODA
G
F
C
Take my hand and take this ring and know that I
Am
G
C/G
will al - ways love you through an - y - thing, yeah,
G
Am
C
G
yeah. And as the years march on like a beat - ing

F
Am
C
Fsus2
G
heart, I will live these words: "till death do us part." 'Cause I have
Fsus2
C
Am
G
nev - er been so sure of an - y - thing be - fore like I am
F
C
G
C/E
in this mo - ment here with you. And now "for
F
C
Am
G
bet - ter or for worse" are so much more than on - ly words, and I pray

Dm
Am
every day will be the proof that I mean
F
C
G
Am
what I say when I say, "I do." Yeah, I mean
F
C
G
Am
C
G
what I say when I say "I do." Yeah,
F
Am7
C
Fsus2
G
yeah.
rit.